SEVENTH FLEET
SUPER CARRIERS

SEVENTH FLEET
SUPER CARRIERS

US naval air power in the Pacific

Tony Holmes

Looking forward over the bow cats of the *Carl Vinson*, aircraft from four squadrons prepare for the first launch at the beginning of another mission. Behind the E-2 of VAW-114 and the F-14 of VF-51 are two A-7Es of VA-27 and 97, and a Tomcat from VF-111 'Sundowners'

First published in winter 1987
by Osprey Publishing Limited
27A Floral Street, London WC2E 9DP
Member company of the George Philip Group

Reprinted summer 1988

© Tony Holmes

British Library Cataloguing in Publication Data

Holmes, Tony
    Seventh Fleet Super Carriers: US naval air power in the Pacific.—(Osprey colour series).
    1. United States. *Navy*—Aviation   2. Airplanes, Military—United States
    I. Title
    623.74'6   VG93

ISBN 0-85045-815-3

Editor Dennis Baldry
Designed by David Tarbutt
Printed in Hong Kong

Front cover
With both Pratt & Whitney TF30-P-412 turbofans in Phase Five afterburner and leading edge slats fully deployed, an F-14A Tomcat of V-111 'Sundowners' launches from the USS *Carl Vinson*. Thanks to the powerful steam catapult, even if the Tomcat's engines failed during the shot it would only leave the deck 5 knots slower, giving the crew enough time to eject

Back cover Originally noted for its futuristic island, which had billboard radars on each surface and a beehive dome on top of it, the USS *Enterprise* emerged from a two-and-a-half year refit with a more conventional-looking superstructure. The small troughs on the front and side of the superstructure hold the Mk 91 fire-control system for the Sea Sparrow SAM system. The first nuclear-powered aircraft carrier in the world, *Enterprise* was commissioned in 1961. In 25 years of eventful service the carrier has seen combat off North Vietnam and, more recently, has patrolled in the Gulf of Sirte during the Libyan crisis, relieving other super carriers in this politically sensitive area

Title pages The USS *Carl Vinson*, or 'Battlestar' as she is known to the carrier's loyal crew. Until October 1986, *Carl Vinson* had been the newest carrier in the Navy but this honour now belongs to her sister ship, the USS *Theodore Roosevelt*. With one of her four elevators down, 'Battlestar' sits peacefully in the waters off Fremantle, Western Australia. A mixed group of A-6s, A-7s and a solitary EA-3B Skywarrior are all parked forward of the bridge

With an area of responsibility covering 52-million square miles, including the entire Indian Ocean and a fair portion of the Pacific, the Seventh Fleet patrols more blue water than any other in the US Navy. The Seventh has also seen more combat since it was established in March, 1943, than any other fleet in any navy in the world. One factor has always been constant in any engagement undertaken by the Fleet; the vital role played by the aircraft carrier. Be it Hellcats or Avengers flying off the USS *Yorktown* or the USS *Enterprise* during the Battle of Leyte Gulf in 1944; Panthers or Banshees from the USS *Lake Champlain* or the USS *Essex* providing vital aerial support for the UN troops in Korea in 1953; or Phantoms and Skyhawks from the USS *Kitty Hawk* or USS *Coral Sea* in 1965 flying strike missions over the jungles of Vietnam, aviators of the Seventh Fleet have completed their duty with skill and bravery.

The Battle Groups of today rely more than ever on the immense power of the 'Super Carrier'. The modern aircraft operated from these vessels provide the vanguard around which American military power at sea is formulated. They are both the offensive and defensive elements of the Seventh Fleet at sea. The cover provided by an air group, which can number up to 90 aircraft depending on

the size of the carrier, enables the US Navy to patrol large areas of ocean many miles from friendly ports and air bases.

This point is particularly pertinent to the Seventh Fleet as they patrol the politically unstable waters in and around the Persian Gulf. This area, known as 'Gonzo Station' to the US Navy crews, has figured prominently in the Fleets operational schedule since the 1979 revolution in Iran. The Tehran hostage crisis, and latterly the escalated attacks on merchant shipping due to the Iran–Iraq war, has led the Seventh Fleet to deploy one Carrier Battle Group, augmented by a similar detachment from the Mediterranean based Sixth Fleet, in the region at all times.

With approximately 80 ships and 440 aircraft, crewed by 60,000 sailors and marines, the Seventh Fleet provides the backbone for the defence of the Western Pacific and Indian Ocean regions. Adding to the fine naval aviation tradition of the Fleet, new aircraft like the F/A-18 Hornet, F-14D 'Super' Tomcat and the A-6F Intruder, along with new Nimitz class aircraft carriers and other naval vessels, ensure that the Fleet motto, 'Ready Power for Peace', will continue to apply through to the 21st century.

Tony Holmes is currently a journalism student in his last year at Curtin University. Aged 20, and born and bred in Western Australia, he lives in the coastal town of Rockingham. He has been interested in aviation for as long as he can remember, a passion instilled in him by his father, who is also an avid aircraft enthusiast. The author has visited many US Navy vessels in the past but the majority of the photographs in this book were taken onboard the USS *Enterprise* (CVN-65) and USS *Carl Vinson* (CVN-70) while both carriers were in the Indian Ocean, and the USS *Ranger* (CV-61) in 1987 when she was cruising in the Western Pacific.

Seventh Fleet Super Carriers would not have been possible without the generous help of Glynis Johns and James Faulkner Channing at the US Consulate in Perth, Lieutenant Bob Anderson, Seventh Fleet Public Affairs in the Philippines, Captain (retired) Ross Underhill USN, the Public Affairs Officers at Atsugi, and the guides who showed the author around the CVs. Finally, thank you to the commanders, officers and crews of the *Enterprise, Carl Vinson, Ranger* and NAF Atsugi for their warm hospitality and valued assistance.

Seventh Fleet Super Carriers was shot using Nikon and Chinon cameras with Tokina and Sigma lenses, loaded with Kodachrome 64.

Dedicated to my family and my lovely Michelle.

The sun is low in the sky as a VF-51 'Screaming Eagles' Tomcat prepares to launch on the first mission of the day. The aircrews' tinted visor becomes essential in these situations.

Contents

Flight deck

A Grumman A-6E TRAM of VMA(AW)-121 'Green Knights' prepares to launch from the USS *Ranger*. The catapult crewman is signalling the all clear to the shooter (next page)

The shooter and his fellow catapult crewmen going about their daily business on the USS *Ranger*

Right A Grumman EA-6B Prowler electronic warfare aircraft of VAQ-134 'Garudas' is shot from one of the waist catapults on the USS *Carl Vinson*. The aircraft's leading edge slats are drooped fully to give the wing as much 'bite' as possible

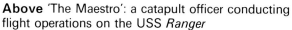

Above 'The Maestro': a catapult officer conducting flight operations on the USS *Ranger*

Right Armed with a mix of Phoenix, Sidewinder and Sparrow air-to-air missiles (AAMs), a Grumman F-14 Tomcat of VF-1 'Wolfpack' is guided onto bow catapult one aboard the USS *Ranger*

Above Guiding their deadly load over the grimy deck of *Carl Vinson*, red shirts push along the hefty weight of six Mk 83 1000 lb (454 kg) bombs. The fuse mechanisms are carried by the officer behind them and screw into the nose of each bomb

Right Flanked by the large landing gear strut of an A-6, an armourer from VA-95 'Green Lizards' works over the pop-out fins which retard the Mk 92 Snakeye bomb he is soon to prime. It is vitally important that the bombs are fitted correctly and securely to the triple ejector racks (TERs) because the forces exerted on the aircraft during launch and recovery can easily wrench loose ordnance from the racks—with potentially disasterous results

Far right The retarding fins of the Mk 92 Snakeye are clearly seen as a red shirt guides 2000 lb (900 kg) of high explosive towards waiting A-6 and A-7 strike aircraft

These newer, smaller all-purpose fire tractors are currently replacing the larger Oshkosh fire trucks on US Navy carriers. This is one of several such vehicles embarked on the USS *Carl Vinson*. Fire is the carriers' greatest enemy

A 'hopper' or 'mule' goes about its business as it tows a recently retrieved aircraft back to the parking area on the stern of *Carl Vinson*

Taking a break from their work inside this Grumman E-2 Hawkeye airborne early warning (AEW) aircraft of VAW-114 'Hormel Hawgs', the brown-shirted plane captain and green-shirted maintenance man peer out of the overhead cockpit windows. It appears that the 'Hawg' emblem is too conspicuous for the Navy's liking and the squadron have been told to scale the piggy down. Never!

The plane captain polishers off the protective
coating on the windshield of the CAG's E-2C
(buno 161344). The receivers underneath the
hinged nose cone form part of the Litton AN/ALR-
73 passive detection system (PDS), which can
detect hostile electro-magnetic emitters at great
distances without giving away the presence or
position of the eavesdropping Hawkeye

At dawn the flight deck of a carrier is a hive of activity. This is a scene aboard the 'Starship' *Enterprise* as the ground crews go about readying the aircraft for the day's first flight operations. The AIM-9L Sidewinder AAMs on the right will shortly be fitted to the Vought A-7E Corsairs of VA-94 'Mighty Shrikes'

Right Leading edge flaps are vitally important on any carrier aircraft as they help to slow down and control the machine before it lands. This is especially true of the Corsair which, because of its relatively small wing area, lands at about 140 knots. Here, green shirts are inspecting the flap hydraulic actuators on Corsair 158016 of VA-97 'Warhawks'

Left A RIO (radar intercept officer) from VF-114 'Aardvarks' pre-flights his F-14 before takeoff. This usually involves a brief but thorough walk-around during which he checks the missile load, any internal work carried out on the aircraft, and the moveable surfaces of the machine. VF-114 are unique in the Navy because they are the only squadron who still wear the old international orange flight suits. This is because the colour matches that of the squadron's emblem, but the 'Aardvarks' are under high-level pressure to change to the standard dark green suit. So far the squadron's only concession to low-vis flight gear is the dark green G-suit

Above Lieutenant Commander Stan O'Connor, callsign 'Steamer', begins the delicate process of fitting into his 'front office'. A graduate of the 'Top Gun' fighter pilot training unit at Miramar, California (note the shoulder patch), 'Steamer' has flown the F-14 for nine years

Left This is what the best dressed A-7 pilots are wearing. The flight helmet is specially fitted and tailored to his individual needs and is decorated with the squadron colours (VA-27 'Royal Maces' in this instance). The hose on his left breast connects with the oxygen system in the cockpit and also contains the microphone lead. On the other side of the suit is his life preserver kit, which contains items essential to the pilots survival should he be forced to eject or crash land his aircraft. The tinted, double thickness visor is especially clear to give the wearer an unobstructed view of the sky around him

The cockpit of the Corsair is tight but comfortable. Visibility is quite good out of the canopy, although the bulk of the ejection seat (a McDonnell Douglas IG-3 Escapac) and the aircraft's broad fuselage spine severely restricts rearward vision

Left With his visor down to block out the effects of the low morning sun, a pilot from VA-22 'Fighting Redcocks' looks out of his cockpit with a glance as sharp and menancing as the tip of his Sidewinder missile. Also visible is the HUD (head-up display) mounted atop the instrument panel. This is the same aircraft/pilot combination featured on the preceding page

Pre-flights take the crew all over their birds to ensure that nothing has been missed by the green shirts. This crewman, standing over the mainspar of his Prowler, seems happy enough

E

CDR PATTERSON

60

AN R MCKINNON
GWT___EVT___

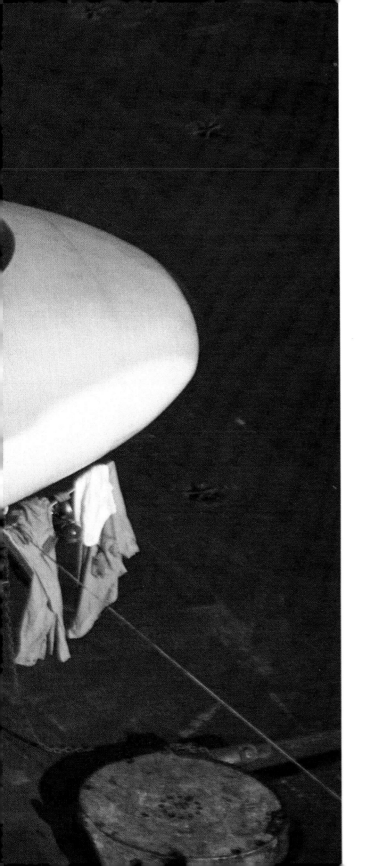

The supreme team: Hawkeye and Tomcat

The large island superstructure of the *Enterprise* towers over the copilot of an E-2 from VAW-117 'Wall Bangers' as he reads through his flight notes before the next mission. The coloured bar under the cockpit is a squadron citation, and the 'Battle E' denotes efficient service over a set period of time

Left A smaller 'Hawg' but a large sash were the colours worn by VAW-114 back in 1983. The Hawkeye squadron was embarked on the *Carl Vinson* during the carrier's inaugural world cruise

Allison T56-A-425 turboprops fired up, a Hawkeye from VAW-117 'Wall Bangers' awaits the arrival of its remaining crew members before being unshackled and directed out to one of the catapults. Inside the large rotodome perched on top of the fuselage is the aircraft's main 'weapon'—the General Electric AN/APS-125 airborne early warning radar. This system was retrofitted to the E-2 fleet from 1976 but it is now being replaced by GE's new APS-138, which is capable of tracking targets over land and sea at distances in the region of 300 miles (480 km) from an altitude of about 30,000 ft (9144 m). A useful adjunct to the Hawkeye's primary role is its ability to recognize and classify enemy electronic emissions

With its wingtip appearing to be too close for
comfort from the parked Intruders ranged over
catapult two, a Hawkeye from VAW-114 'Hormel
Hogs' rockets down the deck of *Carl Vinson* into a
clear blue sky

The pilot of a 'Hormel Hog's' Hawkeye releases the arrestor wire after landing back on *Carl Vinson*. Large power-operated Fowler flaps and long-span ailerons slow the E-2 down considerably before touchdown and also help the pilot to keep this large aircraft on the correct approach angle

Another view of the same VAW-114 E-2C, side number 601, as the outer wings slowly begin to fold back. The large hinge skewers the outer wing panels around until they lie locked parallel with the fuselage

Although there has been talk of low-vising E-2s, the squadrons have not yet been officially told to paint out their colourful badges and national insignia. As one Hawkeye crewman put it 'if the enemy gets through to us then the F-14s haven't done their job and low-vis paint won't save us'. This colourful Hawkeye has the old VAW-117 unit badge on it, worn when the squadron was embarked on the *Enterprise* in January 1983

This page Close-up view of the fuselage of a VAW-116 'Sun Kings' E-2C Hawkeye

Overleaf The C-2A Greyhound carrier onboard delivery (COD) aircraft is a specially designed variant of the E-2 Hawkeye. This particular aircraft from VRC-50 (buno 162150) is one of 39 brand new C-2s ordered by the US Navy to replace the remaining C-1 Traders. The latest C-2s have more powerful engines offering a combined output roughly one-third greater, a new auxiliary power unit (APU) and more efficient avionics

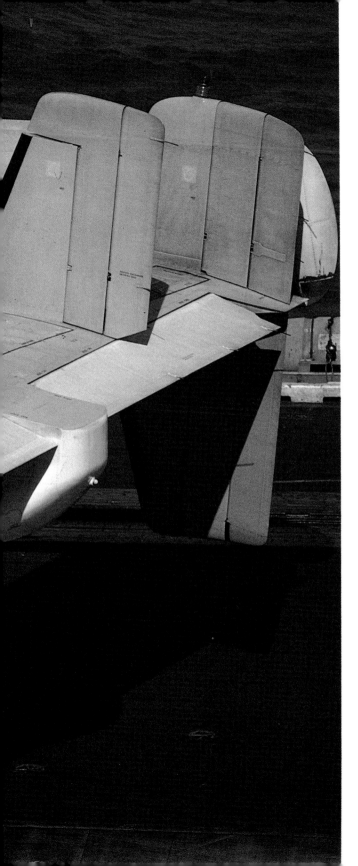

The F-14 Tomcat has a rather simpler set of tail feathers than the C-2 Greyhound at left. Looking a bit faded and perhaps knowing he is soon to swap his proud orange coat for an inconspicuous grey one, this small 'Fighting Aardvark' has cause to feel a little pale

'Go!' The cat officer, still pointing towards the bow of the ship, is obscured by the heat haze and the steam from the catapult as a VF-114 Tomcat roars along the wet and windy deck of *Enterprise*

The changing face of the 'Fighting Aardvarks'.
F-14s from VF-114 sit side-by-side wearing both
the old gloss grey and the new matt low-vis grey
on the flight deck of *Enterprise* on a wintery
morning

The colourful twin-tailed lion and piercing blue rudder speckled with gold stars was once a feature of the Tomcats flown by VF-213 'Blacklions'. This picture was taken onboard the *Enterprise* in January 1983

Left Once a fine looking squadron who wore their black and orange colours with pride, all the members of VF-114 feel sad that the low-vis greys have come into vogue. This F-14 is seen in January 1983 sitting proudly beneath the island on *Enterprise*

After engaging full afterburner on both engines, an F-14 of VF-213 'Blacklions' is launched amid a shower of steam and heat. The aircraft's proximity to the catapult crew is noteworthy

Left In the groove: hook down, gear down, slattery and flappery extended, this VF-213 Tomcat is poised to make a perfect 'trap' on the *Enterprise*. Can you spot the S-3 Viking in the background?

Below This F-14 from VF-51 'Screaming Eagles' is certainly in good hands! In the front seat is the squadron's commanding officer, Commander Jim Robb, and the RIO in back for this mission is CAG (Carrier Air Group Commander), Captain Lyle 'HoChi' Bien. The mottled appearance of the paint below the canopy is interesting

Toting an AIM-9L Sidewinder on the outer glove pylon, a VF-51 Tomcat, side number 101, buno 160675, taxies towards the bow cats. This particular aircraft has had its overall matt grey finish touched up with a bluish shade of a similar colour. Depending on the light conditions pertaining at the time, these low-vis Tomcats can appear to be painted in one of several shades

F-14 '101' of VF-51 rolls past two A-7E Corsairs as it moves purposefully along the flight deck.
Overleaf A flight deck crewman guides the Tomcat onto the launch rail; the catapult shuttle used on the previous launch is travelling up the rail behind him and will soon be attached to the aircraft's nosewheel leg. Note they heavy weathering on the wing due to the wing glove sealing plates rubbing along the surfaces every time sweep is selected. The 'swing wing' confers Mach 2-plus performance and 'dogfight' manoeuvrability across a broad spectrum of speeds and altitudes. The 'Screaming Eagles' have been equipped with the F-14 since the unit pensioned-off its F-4 Phantom IIs in 1978. VF-51 have enjoyed a longer period of continuous service in the Pacific than any other US Navy fighter squadron, and originally flew Curtiss F6C-4 biplanes as VF-3S 'Striking Eagles' back in 1928

Seconds away from the shot, a kneeling white shirt confirms that the engine nozzles are wide open, a sure sign the Pratt & Whitney TF30 turbofans are each producing their maximum advertised thrust of 20,900 lb (9480 kg). The job done by the raised deflector shield can be clearly seen as the heat produced by the engines is blown up into the air

Power personified: a VF-51 Tomcat roars down the deck of *Carl Vinson*. Although the F-14 first flew over 16 years ago, in December 1970, only now is the A model's replacement being designed and tested. The new F-14D is the tangible result of pointed advice from seasoned Tomcat fliers. 'There was an incredible amount of growth potential in the basic F-14A aircraft. The F-14D embodies all of the recommended improvements'. So says Lieutenant Kal 'Wrecker' Felt, a VF-51 Tomcat pilot. Perhaps the most important of these improvements from the pilot standpoint are the new General Electric F110

turbofans. In the current F-14A the pilot has to 'fly the engine' because the TF30 powerplant is vulnerable to flameouts and surges in violent combat manoeuvres. But the F110 will enable the pilot to slam the throttles wide open without fear throughout the Tomcat's entire flight envelope, especially in the high angle of attack/low speed region. Rated at 29,000 lb (13,150 kg) in afterburner, the F110 is also much more powerful and will enable the aircraft to takeoff in military power (i.e. maximum thrust without afterburning) from a carrier deck as a matter of routine

The huge bulk of the F-14 is emphasized by this low-down angle, but it's a beautiful beast! The muzzle blast trough for the 20 mm M61 Vulcan gun can be seen immediately below the nose code. Also visible on this VF-111 'Sundowners' machine is the undernose Northrop TVSU (television sight unit) which gives the RIO a magnified image of a 'bogey' about nine miles (14 km) distant to visually identify it before commencing an attack

F-14s of VF-111 'Sundowners' spring into action on *Carl Vinson* at the start of an air defence mission. With its unique combination of the Hughes AWG-9 radar system and AIM-54 Pheonix missiles, the Tomcat can simultaneously engage six targets flying at heights varying between 50 ft (15 m) and 80,000 ft (24,400 m), and travelling at speeds of up to Mach 2.8 at a range in excess of 100 miles (160 km)—a capability unmatched by any other fighter in the world

Overleaf Looking a good deal smarter than its drab brothers, Tomcat '203', buno 160694, proceeds to its allocated catapult. The crew are wearing highly stylized bonedomes decorated with the famous sunray motif of VF-111

Left The CAG's Tomcat features a small Superman motif under the front cockpit. Nicknamed 'Super CAG' because of his high rank, Captain Ron Zlatoper is attached to VF-111 besides being the commander of Air Wing 15

Above Once a distinguishing feature proudly worn by VF-111, the sharkmouth has disappeared from all their F-14s. Well, almost. This set of gnashers decorated the TVSU bullet of Tomcat '211', buno 161144

Right Back in July 1983, VF-111 were still giving their F-14s the full sharkmouth treatment. This example, side number 207, is also pictured overleaf

Its canopy covered in protective polish, this Tomcat is wearing a curious blend of low-vis national insignia, an overall light grey paint scheme, and the traditional blood red and white fin and sharkmouth so long associated with VF-111

The flight deck crew look on as a Tomcat from VF-
2 'Bounty Hunters' prepares to launch from waist
catapult four on the USS *Ranger*

A pair of VF-2 'Bounty Hunters' head up a line of
Intruders parked on the bow of *Ranger*. The wing
of the F-14 is equipped with an 'oversweep' facility
to maximize parking space

The current tail markings of VF-1 'Wolfpack' and
VF-2 'Bounty Hunters' and, at right, as they were
on the *Ranger* in September 1982

Bomb trucks

The wake of the *Enterprise* forms an impressive
backdrop as an A-6E TRAM Intruder from VA-95
'Green Lizards' lines up for a landing

An Intruder from VMA(AW)-121 'Green Knights', a Marine Corps squadron, hooks the wire and makes a textbook 'trap' on the *Ranger*

'Go that way'. The deck handler at right of picture
directs an Intruder to its parking spot after recovery.
The service life of the A-6E is being extended by
fitting a new composite wing designed by Boeing.
This wing will also be a feature of the forthcoming
A-6F, an extremely advanced upgrade of the
Intruder which is scheduled to enter service in 1990

Apart from the SH-3H Sea King from HS-6 'Indians' running-up in the background, all is quiet aboard the *Enterprise*. The Intruders belong to VA-95 'Green Lizards'. Side number 502 was converted from an A-6A model and like most other A-6Es it incorporates the target recognition attack multi-sensor (TRAM) turret under the nose

The bombadier/navigator makes a signal towards the deck crewman (out of shot). This will be understood to mean, 'Arrestor wire disengaged. Tail hook retracted. Aircraft rotating away'. The heavy weathering of the overall grey paint scheme on this VA-52 'Knight Riders' Intruder is typical

Moments before launch, the catapult crew check the main breaker strut on the Intruder's nose gear leg. This VA-52 A-6E TRAM displays the red paint behind the leading edge slat, a marked contrast to the drab grey covering the rest of the aircraft

A scruffy VA-52 Intruder returns to its parking spot aft. The A-6A entered US Navy service on 1 February 1963 and the first A-6E made its maiden flight on 10 November 1970. The first A-6E TRAM flew in October 1974

The bombardier/navigator in the right-hand seat checks his mission notes as the pilot threads their Intruder towards the bow catapults of *Carl Vinson*. Side number 507 is bombed-up with four 2000 lb (900 kg) Mk 84s slung under a pair of multiple ejector racks (MERs)

Featuring an unusual yellow square marking on the left intake, this A-6E TRAM of VA-145 'Swordsmen' is securely tied down on the *Ranger*

Overleaf A KA-6D tanker of VA-52 'Knight Riders' about to slam onto the deck of *Carl Vinson*. The old-style perforated airbrake from the A-6A sits immediately above the modification seen only on the tanker—the housing for the hose and drogue refuelling line. The flap cut-out, a feature common to all Intruders, is also visible

The Intruder is undoubtedly one of the most versatile aircraft ever operated by the US Navy. This A-6E TRAM of VA-145 'Swordsmen' has a 'buddy' refuelling pack on the centreline and two Snakeyes under each wing

'Hello, I'm an A-7 Corsair. Everything else sucks'.
With its avionics hatch still open and the pilot's
boarding ladder extended, this A-7E from VA-22
'Fighting Redcocks' is being turned-around for its
next mission. The AIM-9L Sidewinder missile
mounted on the fuselage pylon gives the Corsair a
self-defence capability against enemy fighters. This
particular aircraft has a non-standard dayglo ejector
seat warning triangle painted immediately behind
the pilot's name

Left Corsairs also operate as tankers, backing up the dedicated KA-6Ds. A large 'buddy' pack is usually mounted on stations one or eight, balanced by bolting two 300 US gal Aero tanks under the opposite wing. A-7E Corsair, side number 404, buno 159288, from VA-27 'Royal Maces' is rigged with refuelling gear and awaits its turn for launch on *Carl Vinson*

Bombed-up and ready to go, two Corsairs sit secured to catapults one and three while an F-14 is guided between them. The size of the flight deck on *Carl Vinson* is self-evident

All-moving tailplanes neutral, wings folded out, and 500 lb (225 kg) Mk 82 bombs secured to the racks, an A-7E from VA-97 'Warhawks' is guided onto the catapult. The rather mottled appearance of the paint scheme is noteworthy. Although the 'cat men' are paid an extra $100 per month by Uncle Sam it seems a less than adequate reward for working in this intense, dangerous environment

Right Launch! The pilot is pushed firmly back into his seat by G-force as his mount shoots from the deck of *Carl Vinson*. This Corsair is armed with retarded Snakeyes

A perfect recovery: the arrestor wire begins to scurry back after being released by the hook of this well-worn Corsair of VA-27 'Royal Maces'. The wing fold mechanism is just beginning to take effect

Another view of '401', turning now and ready to be parked on the bow. The first A-7E model flew on 25 November 1968 and Vought built a total of 596 for the Navy

The drabness of this Corsair is matched only by the threatening skies in the background. Once a very colourful squadron, VA-22 'Fighting Redcocks' have now also succumbed to the disease which has afflicted nearly all operational aircraft in the Navy— low visibility greys

Now this is more like it! A far healthier VA-22
Corsair in the days when the 'Fighting Cock' was
red. '302' is fitted with a forward looking infrared
receiver (FLIR) pod underwing, used to improve
the aircraft's night attack capabilities. The Navy only
has 91 of these pods and they can only be fitted to
231 specially modified A-7s. The paint scheme is
somewhat rare, being overall light gloss grey

A colourful collection of Corsairs from VA-22 'Fighting Redcocks' and VA-94 'Mighty Shrikes' parked under the gaze of the bridge on *Enterprise* in 1983

Right A Corsair looms over the deck of *Enterprise*, poised for touchdown

Sub smashers

An S-3A Viking anti-submarine aircraft from VS-29
'Screaming Dragonfires' performs an impeccable
landing on *Enterprise*. The aircraft will soon clear
the deck for the next customer 30 seconds behind.
Designed by Lockheed-California, the S-3 was a
joint venture with LTV (Vought) which makes the
wing, engine pods, tail and landing gear. The S-3
prototype flew on 21 January 1972 and the first of
179 service deliveries followed in October 1973

Above A VS-29 Viking (buno 160575) is forced to go around again because the deck is still obstructed by the last arrival. The arrestor hook is locked down and the landing gear, based on the F-8 Crusader's, is also extended

Left An S-3 squadron usually numbers ten aircraft and they provide the primary anti-submarine force with SH-3H Sea Kings in support. These Vikings still look smart in VS-21's traditional grey and white scheme, although their 'Fighting Red Tails' nickname rings slightly hollow today; the blood red lightning bolt which cut along the length of the fin has now been replaced with a lacklustre black outline

Right The 'Fighting Red Tails' looked far more menacing aboard the *Ranger* in 1982. This is the CAG's Viking, complete with rainbow coloured fin tip and 'double nuts' zeros. The hinge line for the folding fin is just above the serial

The 'Screaming Dragonfires' in all their former
glory. VS-29's splendid Viking boat motif has since
shrunk into a smaller grey version

Not a pretty sight. Low-visibility S-3A of VS-29
'Fighting Red Tails' waits for its crew aboard the
Carl Vinson. The large wing hinges reduce the span
by half and are skewed to allow the folded areas to
overlap. Vikings are being steadily upgraded to
S-3B standard, with new avionics and equipment and
provision to launch AGM-84A Harpoon anti-ship
missiles from the wing pylons. The internal weapon
bays can accommodate four Mk 46 torpedoes, four
Mk 82 bombs and various depth bombs or mines

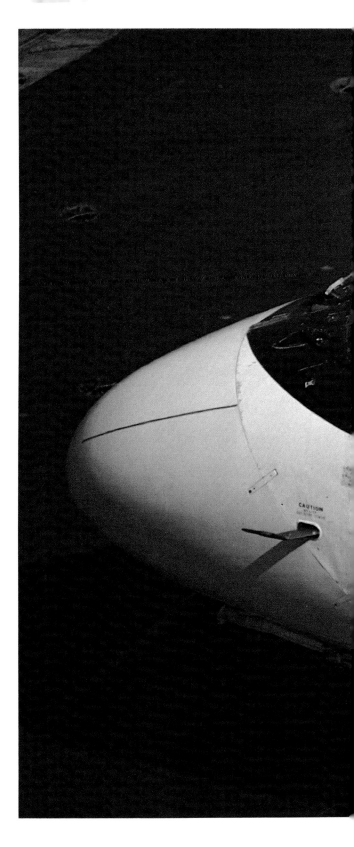

The pilot of a US-3A COD Viking looks out through the heavily tinted windshield. The small slit window immediately behind the cockpit is for the convenience of passengers and is only seen on the six COD Vikings. Based at Cubi Point in the Philippines, VRC-50 operates a mixed fleet of US-3As and C-2A Greyhounds. Because of the large distances involved in flying out to the super carriers of the Seventh Fleet steaming in the Western Pacific or Indian Ocean, VRC-50 is the exclusive operator of this fast, long-range aircraft. Due to the high cost of reopening the Viking production line (closed since 1980), this situation is unlikely to change unless new-build S-3Bs are ordered in quantity

This page A US-3A prepares to depart with a cargo of passengers, priority cargo and mail; the wings are just beginning to unfold. Buno 157995 has two Aero 1D auxiliary fuel tanks mounted under the wing pylons. **Right** 'Miss Piggy' at rest; the fin is only folded if the aircraft has to be struck down into the hangar for maintenance

An S-3A Viking of VS-38 'Red Griffins' unfolds its wings before being launched from the *Ranger*. The moment arm on the wing fold hinge must be considerable

An SH-3H Sea King anti-submarine warfare (ASW) helicopter of HS-14 'Chargers' receives attention before the flight crew get aboard to start the mission. Originally designated HSS-2, the aptly named Sea King was the world's first fully equipped ASW helicopter. Its sensor package includes radar, dunking sonar, sonobuoys (dropped in a precise pattern around the target) and a MAD (magnetic-anomaly detector) 'bird' towed on the end of a cable to help get a fix on a submarine by detecting distortion caused to the Earth's magnetic field. Once located, the sub can be sunk by homing torpedoes or depth bombs carried along the sides of the helicopter

Another HS-14 machine, but this time painted in dreaded low-visibility grey. Despite the flying boat hull and watertight planing bottom, landings at sea are not part of normal operations but these design attributes provide a fair margin of safety in the event of an emergency splashdown. Buoyancy bags are carried in the stabilizing floats

The Sea King became operational in September 1961 and has given the Navy outstanding service ever since. Like the earlier SH-3G, the current SH-3H is also an upgraded conversion from the SH-3A. The Sea King is soon to be replaced by the smaller SH-60B Sea Hawk, also made by Sikorsky, but meanwhile this HS-6 'Indians' example continues to fly from the *Enterprise*. **Overleaf** The plane-guard Sea King (also pictured on this page) lifts off as another HS-6 'Indians' machine goes through a preflight inspection in the background. A Sea King has to be on station alongside the carrier before any launchings can proceed in case a crew is forced to eject during takeoff or landing

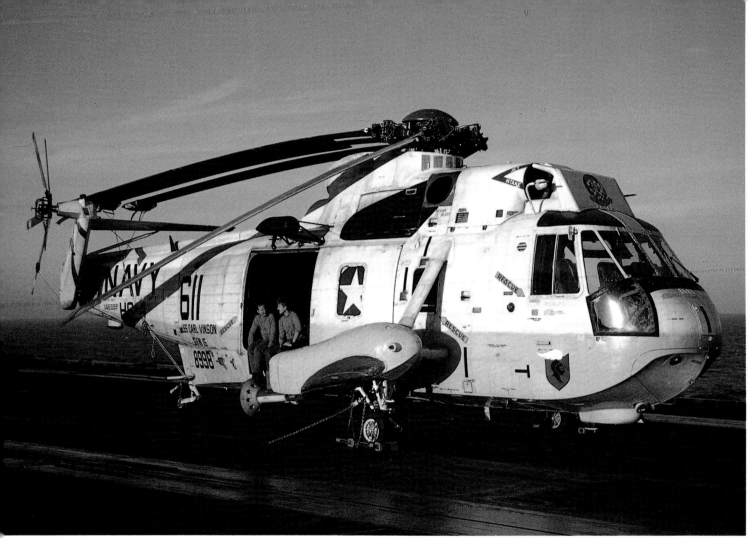

An SH-3H Sea King of HS-4 'Black Knights' provides a convenient sanctuary for two green shirts at the end of the day's flight operations. The Sea King detachment aboard ship usually numbers five aircraft and these machines are used in the general purpose utility role in addition to plane-guard and ASW duties

Another HS-4 Sea King about to recover back on the *Carl Vinson* after an ASW mission. The tail of the MAD 'bird' can be seen protruding from the end of the stabilizing float

Overleaf The cargo-master guides his pilot down onto the deck of the *Carl Vinson*. This HH-46A Sea Knight is from Helicopter Combat Support Squadron Eleven and its Detachment (3) is flying from the Replenishment Oiler USS *Roanoke* (AOR-7)

Hornets at Atsugi

Equipped with ejector bomb racks, a pair of F/A-18 Hornets from VFA-151 'Fighting Vigilantes' stand outside one of the hangars at the Naval Air Facility Atsugi, Japan. **Right** A Hornet from VFA-195 'Dambusters' (left) shares a parking space with its shipmate from VFA-151, also assigned to the carrier *Midway*

The squadron badge of VFA-151 'Fighting Vigilantes' is a new design and bears no resemblance to the former multi-fin flashes which adorned the tails of their F-4 Phantom IIs for many years

Right With the Air Wing soon to embark on the USS *Midway*, VFA-151 practice touch-and-go landings at Atsugi

Above A ground crewman checks fuel cell panels on a Hornet from VFA-192 'World Famous Golden Dragons'. The integral pilot's ladder swings up into the left LEX (leading edge extension) when not in use

Top left The F/A-18 is powered by two closely spaced 16,000 lb (7257 kg) thrust General Electric F404 augmented turbofans. This VFA-195 'Dambusters' example is making its way back to the dispersal area after a routine training flight. Aircraft recognition experts will have spotted the Shinmeiwa US-1 search and rescue flying boat, P-3 Orion and C-2 Greyhound parked in the background

Left Stormy skies, almost the same colour as the aircraft, frame an F/A-18 from VFA-195

Overleaf An impressive line-up of 'Golden Dragons' on the flight-line outside CVW-5's hangar facilities

A head-on view of the Hornet which seems to reveal the aggressive 'sit' of this sturdy multi-mission strike fighter. Downstream of the radar radome is the central aperture for the muzzle of the 20 mm M61 Vulcan gun; the magazine holds 540 rounds. A neat retractable refuelling probe is also situated in the nose

Right Brightly coloured helmet contrasting with his drab VFA-192 'CAG bird', Captain M L Bowman ('Badman') vacates his office after a mission. The Hornet has a large, comfortable cockpit and visibility is excellent

Beam weapons

Affectionately known as 'The Whale', the Douglas EA-3B Skywarrior is an electronic countermeasures (ECM) platform packed with tons of sensors, decoys, jammers and assorted gismos to frustrate enemy radars and communications. Weighing a hefty 82,000 lb (37,195 kg) fully loaded the EA-3B is easily the largest and heaviest aircraft to be seen on a carrier deck. **Above** The roomy cockpit and its commanding view of the flight deck is appreciated by the pilot and navigator. This particular aircraft, buno 146459, assigned to Air Wing Fifteen, was unfortunate enough to get the blowlamp treatment from an F-14 in full afterburner mode before takeoff, which left her with a melted nose and bubbled windows

At 72 ft 6 in (22.1 m), the wing span of the Skywarrior is wider than the F-14's in the fully forward position and this leaves little room for error on landing, even on super carriers like *Carl Vinson*. The EA-3B is the only aircraft in the fleet which still uses the old bridle and brace wires system for launching

After a day's operational flying 'The Whale' from
VQ-1 'World Watchers' is allowed to repose until
the following morning. A small note inside the main
landing gear door reads 'on loan from the
Smithsonian Institute'. This airframe is a young one,
built in 1958; the last new delivery (an A3D-2Q)
occurred in January 1961

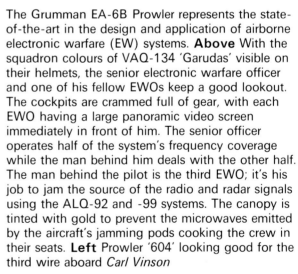

The Grumman EA-6B Prowler represents the state-of-the-art in the design and application of airborne electronic warfare (EW) systems. **Above** With the squadron colours of VAQ-134 'Garudas' visible on their helmets, the senior electronic warfare officer and one of his fellow EWOs keep a good lookout. The cockpits are crammed full of gear, with each EWO having a large panoramic video screen immediately in front of him. The senior officer operates half of the system's frequency coverage while the man behind him deals with the other half. The man behind the pilot is the third EWO; it's his job to jam the source of the radio and radar signals using the ALQ-92 and -99 systems. The canopy is tinted with gold to prevent the microwaves emitted by the aircraft's jamming pods cooking the crew in their seats. **Left** Prowler '604' looking good for the third wire aboard *Carl Vinson*

The Prowler's main offensive weapon, the AIL ALQ-99 high-power noise jamming pod, hangs from the pylon underneath the wing hinge. The bulbous fairing on the fin contains several surveillance dishes, and more antennae are housed in the blisters further down the fin

Space is at a premium on the flight deck and aircraft are parked as close together and as near to the edge of the deck as possible. Prowler '604' seems to have been marshalled into a precarious position, but the deck handler has seen it all before and has the situation well under control

Overleaf The helmet of an EWO from VAQ-134 'Garudas' perched on the windmill propeller which energizes the jammer pod via a Garrett AiResearch ram-air turbine